CELEBRATE GOD'S MIGHTY DEEDS

MY PRAYER BOOK

PAULIST PRESS
NEW YORK, N.Y. GLEN ROCK, N.J.
TORONTO AND MONTREAL

The Prayer Book "Celebrate God's Mighty Deeds" is the English version of "Mon livre de Prière: Célébrons ses Merveilles" written by the Office Catéchistique Provincial. This version was prepared with the collaboration of the National Office of Religious Education, Ottawa, Canada.

NIHIL OBSTAT	Barry McGrory, S.T.D. *Censor Deputatus*
IMPRIMATUR	Gérard-Marie Coderre, D.D. *Bishop of St. Jean-de-Québec, Canada* April 10, 1967
ILLUSTRATIONS	by Rose-Anne Monna
COPYRIGHT	© 1967 by Office Catéchistique Provincial, Montréal Canada
PUBLISHED	IN THE U.S.A.: PAULIST PRESS 21 Harristown Road Glen Rock, New Jersey, 07452 and 304 W. 58th Street New York, N.Y. 10019 IN CANADA: PAULIST PRESS 455 King Street West, Toronto 2B, Ontario and P.O. Box 153, Station R Montréal 10, Québec
PRINTED AND BOUND	by The St. Lawrence Lithographing Limited Montréal 10, Québec

DEAR PARENTS,

THIS PRAYER BOOK was composed in the same spirit as the second-grade catechism, CELEBRATE GOD'S MIGHTY DEEDS, that is, it invites the child to praise and thank God for his gifts.

It will help your child to enter with you into the liturgical renewal; it will permit him to celebrate in the Christian assembly the great deed the Lord has accomplished for us: the eucharist.

In this book you will find:

- some basic texts drawn from the catechism to guide your child's morning and night prayer (pp. 7-11);

- some supplementary texts that he already knows and that will allow him to vary his prayer (pp. 12-15);

- two blank pages on which he can write some prayers of his own choice (pp. 16-17);

- certain prayers from the Mass that will help him to participate better in the eucharistic celebration (pp. 18-49);

- some suggestions to help him celebrate the sacrament of penance (50-56).

You may guide your child in using this prayer book as follows:

- by explaining to him some of the texts of the Mass, you will help him have a deeper understanding of the riches of the eucharistic celebration;

- by helping him during Mass and indicating the pages that correspond to the various parts of the celebration, you will enable him to unite himself to the prayer of the Christian assembly;

• by carefully respecting his choice of texts for prayer you will help your child choose those he wishes to say to the Lord, or make up his own. The suggested texts are examples. The child may write his own prayers on the blank pages reserved for this purpose.

It is hoped that this prayer book will help your child celebrate with great faith the mighty deeds of the Lord.

> *Let us praise and thank the Lord for his love,*
> *and his mighty deeds for the children of men.*
> *Let us celebrate his mighty deeds*
> *in the assembly.*

(Adapted from Psalm 106 [107], 31-32)

CELEBRATE
GOD'S MIGHTY DEEDS

EACH MORNING AND EACH EVENING

Each morning I can choose
any of these prayers:

*I ADORE GOD, THE FATHER,
THE SON AND THE HOLY SPIRIT*

Holy, Holy, Holy

Lord, God of hosts!
Heaven and earth
are filled with your glory.

*WITH ALL CHRISTIANS,
I TELL THE FATHER
OF MY LOVE AND TRUST.*

Our Father

who art in heaven . . .

*WITH JESUS, I OFFER MY DAY
TO GOD OUR FATHER*

Here I am, Father. I have come to do your will!

To you, Lord, we offer the wonderful world!
To you, Lord, we offer the work of our hands!
To you, Lord, we offer the joy of our hearts!

Through Jesus, with him and in him
is given to you, Father almighty,
together with the Holy Spirit,
all honor and glory,
forever and ever. Amen.

I ASK HELP FROM THE HOLY SPIRIT

Holy Spirit, help me to please the Father
during this day, by loving others,
as Jesus loves them.

Each evening
I can choose one of these prayers:

*I PRAISE GOD, THE FATHER,
THE SON AND THE HOLY SPIRIT*

Glory be to God the Father,
and to Jesus Christ our Lord
and Brother.
Glory be to the Holy Spirit,
who lives in our hearts.

                              Alleluia.

*WITH GOD OUR FATHER PRESENT WITH ME,
I THINK ABOUT MY DAY*

- *I thank him . . .*
- *I ask his forgiveness . . .*
- *In my heart I forgive
  anyone who has hurt me;
  then I say:*

   Our Father . . .
   forgive us our trespasses
   as we forgive those
   who trespass against us.

*I TELL JESUS OF MY LOVE
AND TRUST*

Lord Jesus,
you are powerful and good
like God your Father.
I have trust in you.

I GREET MARY

Hail Mary,
full of grace . . .

*I PRAY TO HER FOR ALL
THE PEOPLE IN THE WORLD*

Holy Mary, Mother of God,
pray for us, sinners . . .

On these pages you will find some prayers that you know. You may pray them when you wish: morning, evening, or any time throughout the day.

WE ADORE THE LORD AND WE THANK HIM

Lord, how great and wonderful you are!
Who is like you, in heaven or on earth?

It is right and just to sing your praise, O Lord,
for Jesus Christ, your Son, God made man.

It is right and good to praise and thank you,
Father, for you do mighty deeds in us.

Sing to the Lord a new song
for he has done wonderful things.
He has made known his love
to all the people on earth.

All praise to God the Father be.
All praise, eternal Son, to thee,
whom, with the Spirit, we adore
forever and forever more.

All the earth proclaim the Lord.
Sing your praise to God.

Glory to God in the highest.
And on earth peace to men of goodwill.

Glory be to the Father,
and to the Son and to the Holy Spirit.

Glory and praise to you, Lord Jesus!

You are the Christ, the Son of the living God!

*WE TELL THE LORD
OF OUR LOVE AND TRUST*

My God, you look upon us with love. Alleluia.
And we are full of joy. Alleluia.

My soul is waiting for the Lord;
in him I put all my hope and trust!

Lord, you look upon me;
I am happy and not afraid
because I know you love me.

We belong to you, O God,
we belong to you.

Your Word, Lord, is my joy
and the happiness of my heart.

*WE ASK THE LORD'S HELP
WITH TRUST*

> I treasure your Word in my heart.
> Make me live in your love.
>
> My soul is longing for your peace
> near to you, my God.
>
> We wait in joy, O Lord,
> till you return to take us home;
> we wait in joy, O Lord.
>
> I ask the Lord for only one thing
> and I want it with all my heart:
> that I may live forever in the Lord's house.
>
> Lord, gather in your Church
> all our brothers who live on the earth.

WE CAN SAY
before meals:

> God our Father,
> we thank you for this meal;
> help us to care about the needs of our brothers.

after meals:

> God our Father,
> you have gathered us together around this table;
> gather us again one day in your home in heaven.

WE ASK THE LORD TO FORGIVE US

>Lord, forgive my sins,
>for I have trust in you.
>
>Heal me, Lord,
>for I have sinned against you.
>
>O God of love, have mercy!
>Free me, O God, from my sin.
>>(*24th Week, Grade 1*)

WE PRAY TO THE VIRGIN MARY

>Rejoice, Mary, full of grace.
>The Lord is with you.
>
>You are all beautiful, O Mary,
>like a star that shines at night.
>It was through you that God our Father
>gave us Christ, our living Light.

On these pages you can write other prayers that you make up yourself and that you wish to remember so you can say them to the Lord.

CELEBRATE
GOD'S MIGHTY DEEDS

IN THE EUCHARISTIC ASSEMBLY

1 - Entrance Rite

- Entrance Psalm
- Prayer To Ask Mercy: Kyrie
- Song of Praise: Gloria
- Prayer

Entrance Psalm

All the earth proclaim the Lord!
Sing your praise to God.

Serve you the Lord, heart filled with gladness.
Come into his presence singing for joy.

Know that the Lord is our creator.
Yes, he is our Father; we are his sons.

We are the sheep of his green pasture;
for we are his people; he is our God.

Enter his gates bringing thanksgiving.
O enter his courts while singing his praise.

Our Lord is good, his love enduring;
his Word is abiding now with all men.

Honor and praise be to the Father,
the Son, and the Spirit, world without end.

All the earth proclaim the Lord!
Sing your praise to God.

Psalm 99

Kyrie

We ask the Lord Jesus

Lord, have mercy.

Lord, have mercy.

Lord, have mercy.

Christ, have mercy.

Christ, have mercy.

Christ, have mercy.

Lord, have mercy.

Lord, have mercy.

Lord, have mercy.

Gloria

We sing praise to GOD the Father,
the Son and the Holy Spirit

Glory to God in the highest.

And on earth peace to men of goodwill.

We praise you. We bless you. We worship you.

We glorify you. We give you thanks for your great glory.

Lord God, heavenly King,
God the Father almighty.

Lord Jesus Christ, the only-begotten Son.

Lord God, Lamb of God, Son of the Father.

You, who take away the sins of the world, have mercy on us.

You, who take away the sins of the world, receive our prayer.

You, who sit at the right hand of the Father, have mercy on us.

For you alone are holy.

You alone are Lord.

You alone, O Jesus Christ, are most high,
with the Holy Spirit

In the glory of God the Father. Amen.

2 - Liturgy of the Word

- Reading of the Epistle
- Meditation Song (Gradual)
- Proclamation of the Gospel
- Homily
- Creed
- Prayer of the Faithful

Jesus told his friends:

"HE WHO LISTENS TO YOU IS LISTENING TO ME AND TO HIM WHO SENT ME.
(*Adapted from Luke 10, 16*)

Glory to you, O Lord!

Creed

Because we are baptized,
because we have received the Holy Spirit,
we can say together:

I believe in one God,

> **the Father almighty,**
> **maker of heaven and earth,**
> **and of all things visible and invisible.**

And I believe in one Lord, Jesus Christ,
the only-begotten Son of God.
Born of the Father before all ages.

> **God of God,**
> **Light of Light,**
> **true God of true God.**

Begotten, not made, of one substance
with the Father.
By whom all things were made.

> **Who for us men and for our salvation**
> **came down from heaven.**

And he became flesh by the Holy Spirit
of the Virgin Mary, and was made man.

**He was also crucified for us,
suffered under Pontius Pilate,
and was buried.**

And on the third day he rose again,
according to the Scriptures.
He ascended into heaven
and sits at the right hand of the Father.

**He will come again in glory
to judge the living and the dead.
And of his kingdom there will be no end.**

And I believe in the Holy Spirit,
the Lord and Giver of life,
who proceeds from the Father and the Son.

**Who together with the Father and the Son
is adored and glorified,
and who spoke through the prophets.**

And one holy, Catholic,
and Apostolic Church.

**I confess one baptism
for the forgiveness of sins.**

And I await the resurrection of the dead.
And the life of the world to come. Amen.

Prayer of the Faithful

GOD WILLS ALL MEN TO BE SAVED
(Timothy 2, 4)

We pray to the Lord for all people on earth.
We tell him:

Lord, hear our prayer.

For all who are baptized, we pray to the Lord:

Lord, hear our prayer.

For the pope, bishops, and priests,
    we pray to the Lord:

Lord, hear our prayer.

For our parents, our brothers, our sisters,
    and our friends, we pray to the Lord:

Lord, hear our prayer.

For all those who suffer, we pray to the Lord:

Lord, hear our prayer.

That all men may be saved,
    we pray to the Lord:

Lord, hear our prayer.

>Lord, our refuge and our strength,
>you who inspire all true prayer,
>hear the requests of your Church;
>grant us all that we ask with faith,
>through Jesus Christ our Lord.
>
>**Amen.**

3 - Liturgy of the Eucharist

- **Preparation of the Offerings**
- **Eucharistic Prayer**
- **Communion Rite**

Preface

The Lord be with you.
And with your spirit.

Lift up your hearts.
We have lifted them up to the Lord.

Let us give thanks to the Lord our God.
It is right and just.

Right and worthy it is, fitting and for our good
that in every time and place
our thanks should rise to you, O Lord, holy Father,
almighty and eternal God.

(*Ordinary Sundays*)
Together with your only Son
and Holy Spirit, you are one God, one Lord.
We believe in you and we adore you.

(*Easter time*)
With great joy during this Easter time,
we give you thanks,
for Jesus was put to death for our sins
and has given us life by his
resurrection.

With the angels and saints in heaven,
we sing and proclaim:

Holy, holy, holy, Lord God of hosts.
Heaven and earth are filled with your glory.
Hosanna in the highest.
Blessed is he who comes in the name of the Lord.
Hosanna in the highest.

Consecration

At the Last Supper

Jesus took bread, offered praise and thanksgiving to his Father and gave it to his friends, saying:

"THIS IS MY BODY
WHICH IS BEING GIVEN FOR YOU."

(*Adapted from Luke 22, 19*)

Then, taking a cup of wine, he offered praise and thanksgiving to his Father and gave it to his friends, saying:

"THIS IS MY BLOOD WHICH WILL
BE SHED FOR THE FORGIVENESS OF
THE SINS OF ALL MEN."

(*Adapted from Matthew 26, 27-28*)

At Mass

> Like Jesus the priest takes bread; he gives thanks to the Father in the name of Jesus and says:
>
> ### "THIS IS MY BODY"
>
> Like Jesus the priest takes wine; he gives thanks to the Father in the name of Jesus and says:
>
> ### "THIS IS MY BLOOD"
>
> *and the risen Jesus is in the midst of us offering himself to his Father.*

GOD LOVED THE WORLD SO MUCH THAT HE GAVE HIS ONLY SON SO THAT ALL MEN WOULD BE SAVED THROUGH HIM.

(*Adapted from John 3, 16-17*)

Your holy death,
   O Lord, we remember.   Amen.

Your blessed resurrection
   we proclaim.   Amen.

Your coming in glory
   we await.   Amen.

We praise and thank you,
God our Father,
through your Son Jesus Christ
and with the Spirit of love.
   Amen.

*With the priest we offer Jesus to God
our Father, and through Jesus, all creation
sings the glory of God.*

Here is the prayer the priest says:

>Through Jesus, with him and in him
>is given to you, Father almighty,
>together with the Holy Spirit,
>all honor and glory,
>forever and ever.

We answer together:
AMEN

We offer ourselves with Jesus.

Here I am, Father. I have come to do your will.

As we have learned from the Lord

and according to his command

we dare to say:

Our Father, who art in heaven,

hallowed be thy name;

thy kingdom come;

thy will be done

on earth as it is in heaven.

Give us this day our daily bread;

and forgive us our trespasses

as we forgive those who trespass against us;

and lead us not into temptation,

but deliver us from evil.

Jesus tells us:

"IF YOU COME TO CHURCH TO OFFER YOUR GIFT, AND THERE YOU REMEMBER THAT YOUR BROTHER HAS SOMETHING AGAINST YOU, LEAVE YOUR GIFT AND GO MAKE FRIENDS WITH YOUR BROTHER."

(Adapted from Matthew 5, 23-24)

> Lamb of God, who take away the sins of the world, have mercy on us.
> Lamb of God, who take away the sins of the world, have mercy on us.
> Lamb of God, who take away the sins of the world, grant us peace.

Communion

Jesus said:

> "IT IS MY FATHER WHO GIVES YOU
> THE BREAD OF HEAVEN.
> I AM THE BREAD OF LIFE.
> THE BREAD THAT I WILL GIVE
> IS MY BODY
> FOR THE LIFE OF THE WORLD."

(John 6, 32. 51-52)

Lord, I am not worthy that you should
come under my roof;
speak but the word and my soul will be healed.

THE BODY OF CHRIST.   **AMEN**

> O God our Father,
> you give us the bread of life,
> which is the risen Jesus;
> give us your Spirit, too,
> so that we may remain united in love.
>
> (*Adapted from the Liturgy of the Paschal Vigil*)

We await your return in glory.

Jesus said:
"HE WHO EATS THIS BREAD OF LIFE WILL LIVE FOREVER, AND I WILL RAISE HIM UP ON THE LAST DAY."

John 6, 55

COME, O COME, LORD JESUS!

Apocalypse 22, 20

GO IN THE PEACE OF CHRIST

We give thanks to God

WORK WITH
A GOOD HEART

LOVE ONE ANOTHER

LET YOUR YES MEAN YES

PRAY TO YOUR FATHER

FORGIVE...

*AFTER MASS, JESUS LIVES IN US
BY HIS SPIRIT TO HELP US LOVE THE FATHER
AND OTHERS AS HE LOVES THEM.*

CELEBRATE GOD'S MIGHTY DEEDS

IN THE SACRAMENT OF PENANCE

Holy Spirit, help me

> to understand the words of Jesus,
> to know my sins,
> to be sorry for them with all my heart.

1 I prepare myself

LOVE THE LORD YOUR GOD..

PRAY TO YOUR FATHER

In the morning, in the evening, throughout the day, and especially on Sunday, turn your heart to the Lord. Praise and thank him. Tell him of your love. Ask him for the Holy Spirit to help you love better.

LOVE OTHERS

Respect others. Make them happy. Like Jesus, be good to all. Pray that all men may please the Father.

FORGIVE

To love God with your whole heart, you must forgive others who have hurt you. Then you will be able to say: "Our Father, forgive us as we forgive others."

LET YOUR "YES" MEAN "YES"

Do your best to tell the truth. In this way, there will be more love in your family, in your class.

WORK WITH A GOOD HEART

Try very hard to apply yourself to all that you do, even if you don't feel like it. In this way, you will do the will of the Father.

Prayer of Sorrow

**God our Father, you have loved us first;
you have given us everything in your Son Jesus;
I am sorry for having offended you.
May your Holy Spirit
help me to become better.**

2 I confess

As soon as you come before the priest,
say: **Father, forgive me for I have sinned.**

The priest answers:
> Remember, Jesus Christ is risen.
> He is our Savior.
> Trust in him and confess your sins.

Now tell him your sins:
> **It is _____ since my last confession.**
> **These are my sins: _____ .**

When you have finished telling your sins,
pray in this way:
> **May God our Father forgive me**
> **and make me true to his Spirit.**

Then listen to what the priest tells you in the name of the Lord.
This is how he forgives your sins:
He makes the sign of the cross over you saying:
> And now, I forgive all your sins,
> in the name of the Father and of the Son and of the Holy Spirit.

Answer: **Amen.**

The priest continues:
> May the Spirit of the Lord Jesus keep you one with the Father and one with his family now and forever.

Answer: **Amen.**

At the end, the priest says to you:
> Go in the peace of Christ.

Answer: **Thank you, Father.**
Then go back to your place.

When I go to confession, Jesus, through the priest, gives me the forgiveness of the Father:

3 I give thanks

THIS IS HOW WE KNOW THE LOVE OF GOD FOR US:
GOD SENT HIS ONLY SON INTO THE WORLD
TO MAKE UP FOR OUR SINS,
SO THAT WE COULD LIVE THROUGH HIM.

1 John 4, 9-10

Lord, I thank you with all my heart,
for the great love you have for me.

Psalm 86

4   I want to make up

To make up is to try to love better.

*I do the penance
that the priest has given me.*

*Then I ask the Holy Spirit to help me
to find a way to make up for my sins:*

- *What will I do to love God our Father better?*
- *What will I do to love others better?*

Lord, you do wonderful things for me.
You open my heart
and I am able to hear you.
Here I am, Lord.
I want to do your will.

Psalm 40

I praise and thank you,
Father, Lord of heaven and earth,
for having made known
your secrets
to little ones.

Luke 10, 21